G-6533

Alice Parker's
Hand-Me-Down Songs

Edited by James Heiks

with an introduction by Alice Parker

GIA Publications, Inc.
Chicago

About Alice Parker's Melodious Accord

Melodious Accord, Inc., was founded in 1984 by Alice Parker and her friends, who share the belief that melody is an unparalleled means of communication for human beings. When we use our ears and voices together, we enrich our lives through creating communities of sound, bringing immediate benefits—physical, mental, and spiritual—to all who join in this most participatory of all the arts.

Melodious Accord carries out its mission by presenting concerts, recording, sponsoring SINGS, providing opportunities for advanced study with Alice Parker, and exchanging information through its publications. Further information is available through www. melodiousaccord.org.

Illustrations: Thomas B. Allen
Cover design: Laura Allen

G-6533

Printed in the U.S.A.
ISBN-13: 978-1-57999-386-3
ISBN-10: 1-57999-386-9

Songbook Introduction by Alice Parker

I've never met a two-year-old who couldn't sing and dance at the same time. There are many things that children must learn as they grow older, but no one has to teach them to sing or to respond to music. Why don't we value this native talent more highly? Perhaps just because it's there—and we want to teach them things that our rational minds dictate, that harness their voices to speech, and their bodies to discipline.

We could be encouraging this talent, feeding it time-tested songs loved by generations of singers and dances that have enlivened the feet of peoples around the world. It's really extremely easy to do: if the parents and teachers sing the songs, the children will join in as they have from time immemorial, and a bridge between the generations is built. If, on the other hand, the parents don't sing, or the children only hear the latest "hits" (which are designed to be replaced by next season's favorite), the child is doomed to be lost in the shallow satisfactions of the moment, rather than joining in the world's song.

This collection is designed to be a stepping stone in the effort to bring folksongs back to our children of all ages. These are songs that generations have sung, that express many different moods and emotions, and allow body, mind and spirit to unite in the only art that springs full-grown from our simple humanity. There is a generous serving of nonsense songs, guaranteed to bring a twinkle to the eye and a smile to the lips. These are dances that invite the feet to move, and work songs that recreate the body's rhythms and the mind's release from the efforts of sailing or railroad building. Animal songs are always favorites, as are western songs that recall the slow moving of the cattle or the lonesome vastness of the prairie. And there are spirituals that can turn our thoughts inward to mystery, or outward to shared joy.

This music is far more than what appears on the page. The printed version is just like a recipe: you can't taste it till it's created—and the song doesn't exist till it's sung. Not just that it's sung, but how it is sung is the issue. If you've learned a song from someone who loves it, you remember not just the words and notes but the attitude of the singer: the face and voice and body, the charm which emanates from a song-sharer. This is the quality that brings in the listener—not the deadly correctness of quarter-note precision. The singer must offer the song in a way that invites participation—and rewards it with a smile.

And the real function of song is to unite us as communities of singers. When we laugh together, or mourn together, or dance to gentle or lively strains, we lose our aloneness—we see and hear and touch each other in ways which affirm our place in the human family. Parents and teachers who sing know how easily the mood of a room can be enlivened or calmed by just the right song, and how children can learn the rewards of joint activity in creating something that not one of them can achieve alone. Songs are carriers of cultural values, and a means for expressing our deepest feelings. Children who sing together have learned a skill that lasts for their entire lives, through songs that remain in the memory for consolation and delight. What could be more valuable?

Alice Parker, founder of the group Melodious Accord, is a highly regarded composer, conductor, and lecturer in the field of choral folksongs, hymns, and spirituals.

Artist **Thomas B. Allen** (1928–2004) wrote and illustrated more than a dozen children's books, including *In Coal Country* (a *New York Times* Best Illustrated Children's Book of the Year). He was named Hallmark Professor at the University of Kansas in 1983, and he was later chair of the illustration department at the Ringling School of Art and Design in Sarasota. Allen was known for his colorful portraits of country, bluegrass, and jazz musicians for album covers, including Earl Scruggs and Ray Charles.

Message to students:

This book is yours. It will fit in your backpack, and there is a place on the inside front cover to add your name. Artist Thomas Allen has added a few sketches on some of his favorite songs, but there is also plenty of room for you to draw your own pictures for your favorite songs. Go ahead and take this book with you wherever you go! When you feel like singing, you'll be ready. Do you think you can sing every song in the book? Do you think you can learn every song in the book by heart?

Warning: These melodies get stuck in your head. They never go away. They will be saved forever in the place where you keep your best memories...just like old friends.

Message to parents, teachers, and song leaders:

The idea behind this little book was to give children an affordable songbook they could make their own. Let them write their names on the cover, and encourage them to draw their own illustrations...take it in the car, to the park, to Grandma's house, camping, anywhere...everywhere.

Every folksong in this book has passed the tests of time...and today's fourth grade classroom! They come with this guarantee: The songs will multiply many times the joy and enthusiasm you put into them.

The notation of these wonderful melodies has been simplified. The performance suggestions for tempo and style are meant to inspire the singer to be creative with interpretation, and perhaps elicit a grin from the singer. Please take liberties with them (especially the rhythms) and make them your own. After all, folk music is dynamic—keep it alive!

–James Heiks

James Heiks is Associate Professor of Music at Goshen College in Goshen, Indiana. He also taught kindergarten through high school in Appleton, Wisconsin, for over thirty years.

Alice Parker's Hand-Me-Down Songs

All Night, All Day

With an easy swing

Refrain

All night, all___ day, An - gels watch - ing o - ver
me my Lord; All night, all___ day, An - gels watch - ing o - ver
me. 1. Now I lay me down to sleep,
An - gels watch - ing o - ver me my Lord; Pray the Lord my
soul_ to keep, An - gels watch - ing o - ver me.

Refrain
All night, all day....

2. If I die before I wake,
   Angels watching over me my Lord;
   Pray the Lord my soul to take,
   Angels watching over me.
   Refrain
   All night, all day....

Blow Ye Winds

Heartily   Sea Chantey

1. They ad-ver-tise in Bos-ton town, New York and Buf-fa-lo, Five hun-dred brave A-mer-i-cans, A-whal-ing for to go.— Sing-ing: Blow ye winds of morn-ing, And blow ye winds, heigh ho! Clear a-way the run-ning gear, And blow ye winds, heigh ho!

2. They send you to New Bedford fair,
   That famous whaling port,
   And give you to some strangers there
   To board and fit you out. Singing:
   Refrain
   Blow ye winds....

3. They tell you of the clipper ships
   A-going in and out,
   And say you'll take five hundred whale
   Before you're six months out. Singing:
   Refrain
   Blow ye winds....

4. It's now we're out to sea, my boys,
   The wind comes up to blow;
   One half the watch is sick on deck,
   The other half below. Singing:
   Refrain
   Blow ye winds....

5. The skipper's on the quarter-deck
   A-squinting at the sails;
   When up aloft the lookout sights
   A mighty school of spouting whales.
   Refrain
   Blow ye winds....

Blue-Tail Fly
(Jimmy Crack Corn)

Folk version of *Minstrel Song* attributed to Dan Emmett

Freely

1. When I was young I used to wait On mas-ter and fill up his plate, And pass the bot-tle when he got dry And brush a-way the blue-tail fly. Jim-my crack corn and I don't care, Jim-my crack corn and I don't care, Jim-my crack corn and I don't care, My mas-ter's gone a-way.

2. When he'd ride out in the afternoon
   I'd follow after with a hickory broom,
   The pony being apt to shy
   When bitten by the blue-tail fly.
   Refrain
   Jimmy crack corn....

3. One day he rode around the farm,
   The flies so numerous they did swarm,
   One chanced to bite him on the thigh;
   Devil take the blue-tail fly.
   Refrain
   Jimmy crack corn....

4. The pony jump, he lurch, he pitch,
   He threw my master in the ditch.
   He died and the jury wondered why
   The verdict was: "The blue-tail fly."
   Refrain
   Jimmy crack corn....

5. They laid him under a 'simmon tree.
   His epitaph is there to see:
   "Beneath this stone I'm forced to lie,
   A victim of the blue-tail fly."
   Refrain
   Jimmy crack corn....

Buffalo Gals

Jauntily

1. Buf - fa - lo gals, won't you come out to - night, Won't you come out to - night, won't you come out to - night?

Buf - fa - lo gals won't you come out to - night And dance by the light of the moon?

Refrain

Will you, won't you, will you, won't you come out to - night? Will you come out to - night, won't you come out to - night? Will you, won't you, will you, won't you come out to - night And dance by the light of the moon?

2. As I was walkin' down the street,
   Down the street, down the street,
   A pretty gal I chanced to meet,
   Oh, she was fair to view.
   Refrain
   Will you, won't you, will you, won't you....

3. I stopped her and we had some talk,
   Had some talk, had some talk,
   But her foot covered up the whole sidewalk
   And left no room for me.
   Refrain
   Will you, won't you, will you, won't you....

4. Purtiest gal I ever seen in my life,
   Seen in my life, seen in my life,
   Oh, I wish to the Lord that she was my wife
   And we would part no more.
   Refrain
   Will you, won't you, will you, won't you....

Repeat Verse 1 with Refrain.

Alternative Refrain
Oh, I danced with a dolly with a hole in her stockin'
And her heel kept a-rockin' and her toe kept a-knockin'.
Oh, I danced with a dolly with a hole in her stockin'
And we danced by the light of the moon.

Camptown Races

Stephen C. Foster

At a gallop

1. The Camp-town la-dies sing this song, doo-dah, doo-dah! The Camp-town race track five miles long, Oh, doo-dah day. I come down here with my hat caved in, doo-dah, doo-dah! I go back home with a pock-et full of tin, Oh, doo-dah day. Going to run all night, Going to run all day, I'll bet my mon-ey on the bob-tail nag, Some-bod-y bet on the bay.

2. The long tail filly and the big black horse, doo-dah, doo-dah!
   They flew the track, and both cut across, Oh, doo-dah day.
   The blind horse sticking in a big mud hole, doo-dah, doo-dah!
   Couldn't touch bottom with a ten-foot pole, Oh, doo-dah day.
   Refrain
   Going to run all night....

3. See them fly on a ten-mile heat, doo-dah, doo-dah!
   Around the track, and then repeat, Oh, doo-dah day.
   I win my money on the bob-tail nag, doo-dah, doo-dah!
   I keep my money in an old towbag, Oh, doo-dah day.
   Refrain
   Going to run all night....

4. Old muley cow came on the track,
        doo-dah, doo-dah!
   The bob-tail threw her over his back,
        Oh, doo-dah day.
   Then flew along like a railroad car,
        doo-dah, doo-dah!
   Like running a race with a shooting star,
        Oh, doo-dah day.
   Refrain
   Going to run all night....

The Colorado Trail

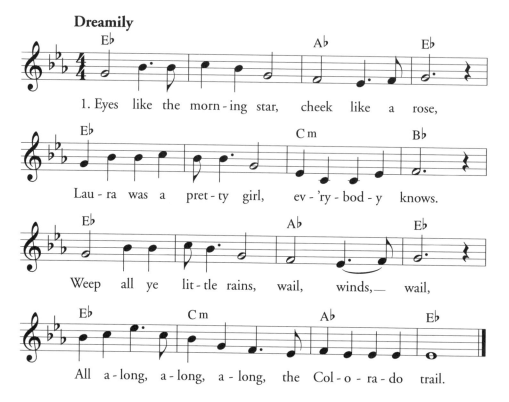

Dreamily

1. Eyes like the morn-ing star, cheek like a rose,

Lau-ra was a pret-ty girl, ev-'ry-bod-y knows.

Weep all ye lit-tle rains, wail, winds,— wail,

All a-long, a-long, a-long, the Col-o-ra-do trail.

2. Seems like only yesterday, I heard her sigh,
   "Never will we meet again," then we said good-bye,
   Weep all ye little rains, wail, winds, wail,
   All along, along, along, the Colorado trail.

3. Many the years have passed, riding the range,
   Many are the memories, time can never change,
   Weep all ye little rains, wail, winds, wail,
   All along, along, along, the Colorado trail.

4. Out on the mountain side, aspen and pine,
   Thinkin' of my Laurie gal, how she was mine,
   Weep all ye little rains, wail, winds, wail,
   All along, along, along, the Colorado trail.

Do, Lord, Remember Me

With spirit
Refrain

American Negro Gospel Song

Do, Lord, oh do, Lord, oh do re - mem - ber me;

Do, Lord, oh do, Lord, oh do re - mem - ber me.

Do, Lord, oh do, Lord, oh do re - mem - ber me;

Do, Lord, re - mem - ber me.———

1. When I'm cros - sing Jor - dan, oh do re - mem - ber me;

When I'm cros - sing Jor - dan, oh do re - mem - ber me.

When I'm cros - sing Jor - dan, oh do re - mem - ber me;

Do, Lord, re - mem - ber me.———

Refrain
Do, Lord, oh do, Lord....

2. When I've got no friends at all, oh do remember me;
   When I've got no friends at all, oh do remember me.
   When I've got no friends at all, oh do remember me;
   Do, Lord, remember me.
   Refrain
   Do, Lord, oh do, Lord....

3. When I'm scared and lonely, Lord, oh do remember me;
   When I'm scared and lonely, Lord, oh do remember me.
   When I'm scared and lonely, Lord, oh do remember me;
   Do, Lord, remember me.
   Refrain
   Do, Lord, oh do, Lord....

Down the River

Energetically

American Play-Party Song

1. The riv-er is up, and the chan-nel is deep, The wind is stead-y and strong;— Oh, won't we have a jol-ly good time As we go sail-ing a-long.

Refrain

Down the riv-er, oh, down the riv-er, Oh, down the riv-er we go!— Down the riv-er, oh, down the riv-er, Oh, down the O-hi-o!—

2. The river is up, and the channel is deep,
   The wind is steady and strong;
   The waves do splash from shore to shore
   As we go sailing along.
   Refrain
   Down the river....

16

The Erie Canal

At a confident walking tempo

1. I've got a mule, her name is Sal,
She's a good old work-er and a good old pal,
Fif-teen miles on the Er-ie Ca-nal.— We've
Fif-teen miles on the Er-ie Ca-nal.—
hauled some bar-ges in our day, Filled with lum-ber,
coal, and hay, And we know ev-'ry inch of the way From
Al-ba-ny— to— Buf-fa-lo.— Low bridge,

Refrain

ev-'ry-bod-y down! Low bridge, for we're com-ing to a town! And you'll
al-ways know your neigh-bor, you'll al-ways know your pal, If you've
ev-er nav-i-gat-ed on the Er-ie Ca-nal.—

2. We'd better get along on our way, old pal,
   Fifteen miles on the Erie Canal.
   'Cause you bet your life I'd never part with Sal,
   Fifteen miles on the Erie Canal.
   We've hauled some barges...
   Refrain
   Low bridge, ev'rybody down....

3. Get up there, mule, here comes a lock;
   We'll make Rome 'bout six o'clock.
   One more trip and back we'll go,
   Right back home to Buffalo.
   We've hauled some barges...
   Refrain
   Low bridge, ev'rybody down....

The Fox

Nimble-footed

1. The fox went out on a chil - ly night And he prayed to the moon to give him light, For he'd man - y miles to go that night Be - fore he reached the town - o, town - o, town - o; For he'd man - y miles to go that night Be - fore he reached the town - o.

2. He ran till he came to the farmer's bin,
   Where the ducks and the geese were kept penned in.
   "A couple of you will grease my chin
   Before I leave this town-o,
      town-o, town-o;
   A couple of you will
      grease my chin
   Before I leave this
      town-o."

3. First he caught the grey goose by the neck,
   Then he swung a duck across his back.
   And he didn't mind the quack, quack, quack,
   Or their legs all dangling down-o, down-o, down-o;
   And he didn't mind the quack, quack, quack,
   Or their legs all dangling down-o.

4. Then old mother Giggle-Gaggle jumped out of bed,
   Out of the window she popped her head,
   Crying, "John! John! The grey goose is gone
   And the fox is in the town-o, town-o, town-o;"
   Crying, "John! John! The grey goose is gone
   And the fox is in the town-o!"

5. Then John, he ran to the top of the hill,
   Blew his horn both loud and shrill;
   The fox, he said, "I better go with my kill
   Or they'll soon be on my tail-o, tail-o, tail-o;"
   The fox, he said, "I better go with my kill
   Or they'll soon be on my tail-o."

6. He ran till he came to his warm den,
   There were the little ones, eight, nine, ten.
   They said, "Daddy, better go back again,
   'Cause it must be a wonderful town-o, town-o, town-o;"
   They said, "Daddy, better go back again,
   'Cause it must be a wonderful town-o."

7. Then the fox and his wife, without any strife,
   Cut up the goose with a fork and knife;
   They never ate such a dinner in their life
   And the little ones chewed on the bones-o, bones-o, bones-o;
   They never ate such a dinner in their life
   And the little ones chewed on the bones-o.

Frog Went A-Courtin'

Relaxed, with style *Virginia*

1. Frog went a-court-in' and he did ride, M-hm, M-hm, Frog went a-court-in' and he did ride, M-hm, M-hm, Frog went a-court-in' and he did ride, Sword and pis-tol by his side, M-hm.

2. Rode right to Miss Mouse's hall, M-hm, M-hm.... *(repeat three times)*
   Where he most tenderly did call, M-hm.

3. Said he, "Miss Mouse, are you within?" M-hm, M-hm....
   "Yes, kind sir, I sit and spin." M-hm.

4. He took Miss Mousie on his knee, M-hm, M-hm....
   Said, "Miss Mouse, will you marry me?" M-hm.

5. "Without my Uncle Rat's consent, M-hm, M-hm....
   I wouldn't marry the President." M-hm.

6. Then Uncle Rat he soon comes home, M-hm, M-hm....
   "Who's been here since I've been gone?" M-hm.

7. "A pretty little dandy man," says she, M-hm, M-hm....
   "Who swears he wants to marry me." M-hm.

8. "Where shall the wedding breakfast be?" M-hm, M-hm....
   "Way down yonder in a hollow tree." M-hm.

9. What shall the wedding breakfast be?" M-hm, M-hm....
"A fried mosquito and a black-eyed pea." M-hm.

10. "Who will make the wedding gown?" M-hm, M-hm....
"Old Miss Rat from Pumpkin Town." M-hm.

11. Then Uncle Rat gave his consent, M-hm, M-hm....
And that's the way the wedding went, M-hm.

12. First to come in was a flying moth, M-hm, M-hm....
She laid out the table cloth, M-hm.

13. Next to come in was a Juney bug, M-hm, M-hm....
Carrying a water jug, M-hm.

14. Next to come in was Mr. Coon, M-hm, M-hm....
Waving about a silver spoon, M-hm.

15. Next to come in was a bumberly bee, M-hm, M-hm....
Set his fiddle on his knee, M-hm.

16. Next to come in was a nimble flea, M-hm, M-hm....
Danced a jig with the bumberly bee, M-hm.

17. Next to come in was Missus Cow, M-hm, M-hm....
Tried to dance but didn't know how, M-hm.

18. Next to come in was a little black tick, M-hm, M-hm....
Ate so much it made him sick, M-hm.

19. Next to come in was Doctor Fly, M-hm, M-hm....
Said Mister Tick would surely die, M-hm.

20. Next to come in was a big black snake, M-hm, M-hm....
Passing 'round the wedding cake, M-hm.

21. Frog and mouse, they went to France, M-hm, M-hm....
And that's the end of this romance, M-hm.

22. Little piece of cornbread lying
on the shelf, M-hm, M-hm....
If you want any more you can
sing it yourself, M-hm.

Git Along Little Dogies

Lazily

1. As I was a - rid - in' one morn - in' for plea - sure, I

spied a cow - punch - er a - rid - in' a - long. His

hat was throwed back and his spurs was a - jing - lin', And

as he ap - proached he was sing - in' — this song.

Refrain

Whoo - pee ti - yi - yo, — git a - long lit - tle

do - gies, It's your mis - for - tune and none of my —

own; Whoo - pee ti - yi - yo, git a - long lit - tle do - gies, You

know that Wy - om - ing's gon - na be your new home.

2. Early in the springtime we'll round up the dogies,
   We'll slap on their brands and we'll bob off their tails.
   We'll round up our horses, load up the chuck wagon,
   Then throw those little dogies upon the trail.
   Refrain
   Whoopee ti-yi-yo....

3. It's whooping and yelling and driving the dogies,
   Oh how I wish that you would go on.
   It's whooping and punching and go on, little dogies,
   For you know Wyoming's gonna be your new home.
   Refrain
   Whoopee ti-yi-yo....

Ground Hog

Skedaddle!

1. Wet up your knife and whis-tle up your dog,
Wet up your knife and whis-tle up your dog, We're
go-in' to the hol-ler to catch a ground hog.
Ground hog!—

2. Too many rocks and too many logs, *(2 times)*
Too many rocks to catch a ground hog.
Ground hog!

3. Here he comes all in a whirl, *(2 times)*
The biggest ground hog in the whole wide world.
Ground hog!

4. The children screamed and the
   children cried, *(2 times)*
Too They love ground hog all
   cooked and fried!
Ground hog!

Ifca's Castle

A steady stroll

Czech Round

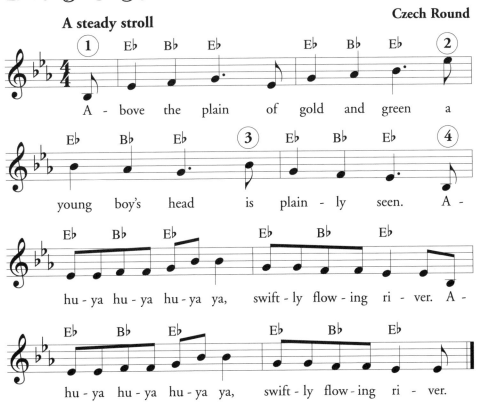

A - bove the plain of gold and green a

young boy's head is plain - ly seen. A -

hu - ya hu - ya hu - ya ya, swift - ly flow - ing ri - ver. A -

hu - ya hu - ya hu - ya ya, swift - ly flow - ing ri - ver.

He's Got the Whole World in His Hands

Firmly and deliberately

Refrain

He's got the whole world in His hands; He's got the whole wide world in His hands; He's got the whole world in His hands; He's got the whole world in His hands. 1. He's got the earth and sky— in His hands; He's got the night and day— in His hands; He's got the sun and moon in His hands; He's got the whole world in His hands.

2. He's got the land and sea in His hands;
   He's got the wind and rain in His hands;
   He's got the spring and fall in His hands;
   He's got the whole world in His hands.
   Refrain
   He's got the whole world....

3. He's got you and me, Brother, in His hands;
   He's got you and me, Sister, in His hands;
   He's got ev'rybody here, in His hands;
   He's got the whole world in His hands.
   Refrain
   He's got the whole world....

Home on the Range

Easy does it

1. Oh, give me a home where the buf - fa - lo roam, Where the

deer and the an - te - lope play;— Where sel - dom is heard a dis -

cour - ag - ing word, And the skies are not cloud - y all day.

Refrain

Home, home on the range,— Where the deer and the an - te - lope

play,— Where sel - dom is heard a dis - cour - ag - ing word And the

skies are not cloud - y all day.—

2. How often at night when the heavens are bright
   With the light from the glittering stars,
   Have I stood there amazed and asked as I gazed
   If their glory exceeds that of ours.
   Refrain
   Home, home on the range....

The Instruments

With confidence

arr. Julius G. Herford

I've Been Working on the Railroad

Start at a steady trudge, end lickety-split

I've been work-ing on the rail-road all the live-long day; I've been work-ing on the rail - road just to pass the time a - way. Don't you hear the whis-tle blow-ing? Rise up so ear-ly in the morn. Don't you hear the cap-tain shout-ing, "Di - nah, blow your horn!" Di - nah won't you blow, Di - nah won't you blow, Di - nah won't you blow your horn?

The Keeper Would A-Hunting Go

Steadily

English Folk Song

1. The keep-er would a-hunt-ing go, And un-der his coat he car-ried a bow, All for to shoot at a mer-ry lit-tle doe A-mong the leaves so— green, O. Jack-ie boy! *Mas-ter!* Sing ye well? *Ver-y well!* Hey down! *Ho down!* Der-ry, der-ry down, **A-mong the leaves so— green, O.** To my hey down, down, *To my ho down, down.* Hey down! *ho down!* Der-ry, der-ry down, **A-mong the leaves so— green, O.**

2. The first doe she did cross the plain,
   The keeper fetched her back again,
   Where she is now she may remain
   Among the leaves so green, O.
   Refrain
   Jackie boy....

3. The second doe she did cross the brook;
   The keeper fetched her back with his crook;
   Where she is now you may go and look
   Among the leaves so green, O.
   Refrain
   Jackie boy....

4. The third doe she ran over the plain;
   But he with his hounds did turn her again,
   And it's there he did hunt in a merry, merry vein
   Among the leaves so green, O.
   Refrain
   Jackie boy....

Kookaburra

With joy   **Australian Round**

(1) Kook - a - bur - ra sits on an old gum tree;—

(2) Mer - ry, mer - ry king of the bush is he.—

(3) Laugh, Kook - a - bur - ra, laugh, Kook - a - bur - ra,

(4) Gay your life must be.

Michael, Row the Boat Ashore

Under full sail

Spiritual

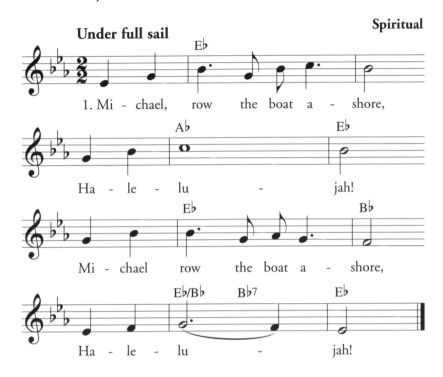

1. Mi - chael, row the boat a - shore,
Ha - le - lu - jah!
Mi - chael row the boat a - shore,
Ha - le - lu - jah!

2. Michael's boat's a music boat, Hallelujah! *(2 times)*

3. Brother, help to trim the sail, Hallelujah! *(2 times)*

4. Jordan River is chilly and cold,
   Hallelujah!
   Chills the body but not the soul,
   Hallelujah!

5. The river is deep and the river is wide,
   Hallelujah!
   Milk and honey on the other side,
   Hallelujah!

6. Michael, row the boat ashore,
   Hallelujah! *(2 times)*

My Bonnie

Wistfully

1. My Bon - nie lies ov - er the o - cean,— My Bon - nie lies o - ver the sea,— My Bon - nie lies o - ver the o - cean.— — O bring back my Bon - nie to me.—

Refrain

Bring back, bring back, O bring back my Bon - nie to me, to me; Bring back, bring back, O bring back my Bon - nie to me.—

2. O blow, ye winds, over the ocean,
   And blow, ye winds, over the sea,
   O blow, ye winds, over the ocean,
   And bring back my Bonnie to me.
   Refrain
   Bring back....

Old Blue

With a heavy heart

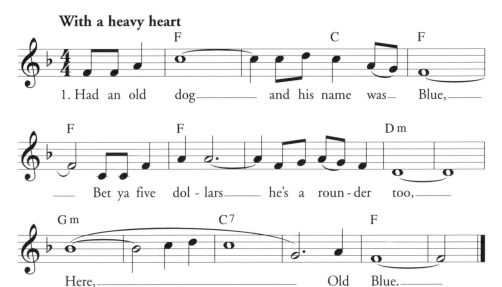

1. Had an old dog_____ and his name was__ Blue,_____

_____ Bet ya five dol - lars_____ he's a roun - der too,_____

Here,_____ Old Blue._____

2. Blue come a-runnin' when I blow my horn,
   Blue come a-runnin' through the yellow corn,
   Here - - - Old Blue!

3. Blue got sick and very thin,
   Called the doctor to come right then,
   Here - - - Old Blue!

4. Doctor came, and he come in a run,
   Said Old Blue, your huntin's done,
   Here - - - Old Blue!

5. Old Blue died and he died mighty hard,
   Shook the ground in my back yard,
   Here - - - Old Blue!

6. When I get to heaven know what I'll do,
   I'll take my horn, and I'll blow for Blue:
   Here - - - Old Blue!

Old Dan Tucker

Raucously

United States

1. Old Dan Tuck-er was a might-y man, Washed his face in a fry-in' pan, Combed his head with a wa-gon wheel, Died with a tooth-ache in his heel.

Refrain

Git out the way, old Dan Tuck-er, You're too late to get your sup-per. Sup-per's o - ver and din - ner's cook-in', Old Dan Tuck-er just stand-in' there look-in'.———

2. I come to town the other night,
   To hear the noise and see the fight.
   The watchman he was a-runnin' around,
   Cryin', "Old Dan Tucker's come to town."
   Refrain
   Git out the way....

3. Old Dan Tucker come to town,
   Riding a billygoat, leading a hound.
   Hound he barked, the billygoat jumped,
   Throwed Dan straddle of a stump.
   Refrain
   Git out the way....

4. Old Dan Tucker clumb a tree
   His Lord and Master for to see;
   The limb it broke, Dan got a fall,
   Never got to see his Lord at all.
   Refrain
   Git out the way....

5. Old Dan Tucker, he came to town,
   Swinging the ladies 'round and 'round;
   First to the right and then to the left,
   And then to the one that you love best.
   Refrain
   Git out the way....

Old Texas

With an amble

Cowboy Song

1. I'm goin' to leave_____ old__ Tex - as now,_____

— They've got no use_____ for the long horn cow.——

— They've plowed and fenced_____ my— cat - tle range,——

— And the peo - ple there_____ are— all so strange.——

2. I'll take my horse, I'll take my rope,
   And I'll hit the trail upon a lope;
   I'll bid Adios to the Alamo,
   And I'll turn my head toward Mexico.

3. I'll make my home on the wide, wide range,
   For the people there are not so strange.
   The hard, hard ground shall be my bed,
   And my saddle seat shall hold my head.

4. And when I waken from my dreams,
   I'll eat my bread and my sardines,
   And when my job on earth is done,
   I'll take my chance with the Holy One.

5. I'll tell Saint Peter that I know
   A cowboy's soul ain't white as snow,
   But in that far-off cattle land,
   He sometimes acted like a man.

Once an Austrian Went Yodeling

Verse like a waltz, refrain like a jig

1. Once an Aus - tri - an went yo - del - ing On a moun - tain so
2. Once an Aus - tri - an went yo - del - ing On a moun - tain so

high, When he met with an av - a - lanche In - ter -
high, When he met with a ski - er In - ter -

rup - ting his cry. } Oh, lay - dee
rup - ting his cry. }

Yo - del - lay - hit - tee, A - yo - del - lay - cuck - oo, cuck - oo,

1. Rum - ble rum - ble)
2. {Rum - ble rum - ble {   Yo - del - lay - hit - tee - a - lo.
   {Whoosh!

3. Once an Austrian went yodeling
   On a mountain so high,
   When he met with a St. Bernard
   Interrupting his cry.

   Refrain
   Oh, lay-dee
   (rapid hand-patting of knees,
   like galloping)
   Yodel-lay-hittee,
   (pat, clap, finger-snap)
   A-yodel-lay-cuckoo, cuckoo,
   (pat, clap, snap-snap)
   Rumble rumble
   (hands rotate like wheels turning,
   for avalanche)
   Whoosh!
   (hand makes swooping, roller-
   coaster movement for skier)
   Arf arf
   (hands up in begging position
   for St. Bernard)
   Yodel-lay-hittee-a-lo.

4. Once an Austrian went yodeling
   On a mountain so high,
   When he met with a grizzly bear
   Interrupting his cry.

   (continue hand motions in each verse)

   Refrain
   Oh, lay-dee
   Yodel-lay-hittee,
   A-yodel-lay-cuckoo, cuckoo,
   Rumble rumble
   Whoosh!
   Arf arf
   Rargh!
   (hands up with fingers like claws,
   in a menacing position, for
   grizzly bear)
   Yodel-lay-hittee-a-lo.

5. Once an Austrian went yodeling
   On a mountain so high,
   When he met with a milking maid
   Interrupting his cry.

   Refrain
   Oh, lay-dee
   Yodel-lay-hittee,
   A-yodel-lay-cuckoo, cuckoo,
   Rumble rumble
   Whoosh!
   Arf arf
   Rargh!
   Psst Psst,
   (hands alternate in milking
   motion)
   Yodel-lay-hittee-a-lo.

6. Once an Austrian went yodeling
   On a mountain so high,
   When he met with a dinosaur
   Interrupting his cry.

   Refrain
   Oh, lay-dee
   Yodel-lay-hittee,
   A-yodel-lay-cuckoo, cuckoo,
   Rumble rumble
   Whoosh!
   Arf arf
   Rargh!
   Psst Psst,
   Eeeeeeeeeeeeeee!
   (everyone shrieks wildly and
   falls on the ground in a heap)

Sandy Land

American Singing Game

Happily

1. Make my liv-ing in sand-y land, Make my liv-ing in sand-y land, Make my liv-ing in sand-y land, La-dies, fare you well.

2. Raise my taters in sandy land,
Raise my taters in sandy land,
Raise my taters in sandy land,
Ladies, fare you well.

3. Keep on digging in sandy land,
Keep on digging in sandy land,
Keep on digging in sandy land,
Ladies, fare you well.

Sarasponda

Dutch Spinning Song

Start slowly...repeat faster and faster until you fall over!

Sa - ra - spon - da, Sa - ra - spon - da, Sa - ra - spon - da, Ret - set - set!

Sa - ra - spon - da, Sa - ra - spon - da, Sa - ra - spon - da, Ret - set - set!

Ah - do - ray - oh! Ah - do - ray - boom - day - oh!

Ah - do - ray - boom - day, Ret - set - set! A - say - pa - say - oh!

The Shanty Boys in the Pine

Lumberjack Song

Slow sawing on a two-man saw

1. Come all ye jol - ly shan - ty boys, come lis - ten to my

song;___ It's all a - bout the shan - ties and

how they get a - long.___ They are a jol - ly

crew of boys, so mer - ry and so fine,___ Who

wile a - way the win - ters a - cut - ting down the pine.___

2. The coppers and the sawyers,
   they lay the timber low,
The skidders and the swampers,
   they holler to and fro,
And then there come the loaders,
   before the break of day;
Come load up the teams, boys,
   and to the woods away.

3. The broken ice is floating
and sunny is the sky;
Three hundred big and strong men
are wanted on the drive.
With cant hooks and with jampikes
these noble men do go,
And risk their lives each springtime
on some big stream you know.

She'll Be Coming 'Round the Mountain

American Folk Song

2. She'll be driving six white horses when she comes. (Whoa, back!)
   She'll be driving six white horses when she comes. (Whoa, back!)
   She'll be driving six white horses,
   She'll be driving six white horses,
   She'll be driving six white horses when she comes. (Whoa, back!)
                                                    (Toot! Toot!)

3. Oh, we'll all go out to meet her when she comes. (Hi, babe!)
   Oh, we'll all go out to meet her when she comes. (Hi, babe!)
   Oh, we'll all go out to meet her,
   Oh, we'll all go out to meet her,
   Oh, we'll all go out to meet her when she comes. (Hi, babe!)

                                                  (Whoa, back!)
                                                  (Toot! Toot!)

4. Oh, we'll kill the old red rooster when she comes. (Hack! Hack!)
   Oh, we'll kill the old red rooster when she comes. (Hack! Hack!)
   Oh, we'll kill the old red rooster,
   Oh, we'll kill the old red rooster,
   Oh, we'll kill the old red rooster when she comes. (Hack! Hack!)

                                                  (Hi, babe!)
                                                (Whoa, back!)
                                                (Toot! Toot!)

5. Oh, we'll all have chicken and dumplings when she comes. (Yum! Yum!)
   Oh, we'll all have chicken and dumplings when she comes. (Yum! Yum!)
   Oh, we'll all have chicken and dumplings,
   Oh, we'll all have chicken and dumplings,
   Oh, we'll all have chicken and dumplings when she comes. (Yum! Yum!)

                                                  (Hack! Hack!)
                                                (Hi, babe!)
                                                (Whoa, back!)
                                                (Toot! Toot!)

There's a Hole in the Middle of the Sea

Silly

1. There's a   hole   in the   mid-dle of the   sea.   There's a
2. There's a   { log   in the / hole   in the }   mid-dle of the   sea.   There's a

hole   in the   mid-dle of the   sea.   There's a hole,   there's a
{ log   in the / hole   in the }   mid-dle of the   sea.   There's a log,   there's a

hole,   There's a   hole   in the mid-dle of the   sea.
log,   There's a   log   in the mid-dle of the   sea.

3. There's a bump
     on the log
        in the hole
           in the middle of the sea....

4. There's a frog
     on the bump
        on the log
           in the hole
              in the middle of the sea....

5. There's a fly
　　　on the frog
　　　　　on the bump
　　　　　　　on the log
　　　　　　　　　in the hole
　　　　　　　　　　　in the middle of the sea....

6. There's a wing
　　　on the fly
　　　　　on the frog
　　　　　　　on the bump
　　　　　　　　　on the log
　　　　　　　　　　　in the hole
　　　　　　　　　　　　　in the middle of the sea....

7. There's a flea
　　　on the wing
　　　　　on the fly
　　　　　　　on the frog
　　　　　　　　　on the bump
　　　　　　　　　　　on the log
　　　　　　　　　　　　　in the hole
　　　　　　　　　　　　　　　in the middle of the sea....

This Little Light of Mine

Spiritual

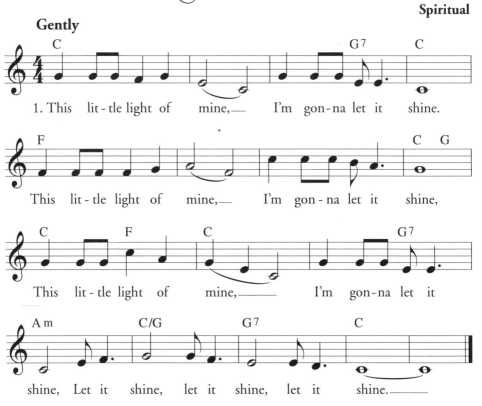

Gently

C   G7   C

1. This lit-tle light of mine,— I'm gon-na let it shine.

F   C   G

This lit-tle light of mine,— I'm gon-na let it shine,

C   F   C   G7

This lit-tle light of mine,———— I'm gon-na let it

Am   C/G   G7   C

shine, Let it shine, let it shine, let it shine.———

2. Ev'rywhere I go, I'm gonna let it shine, *(3 times)*
   Let it shine, let it shine, let it shine.

3. All around my home, I'm gonna let it shine, *(3 times)*
   Let it shine, let it shine, let it shine.

4. All around the world, I'm gonna
      let it shine, *(3 times)*
   Let it shine, let it shine, let it shine.

5. All through the night, I'm gonna
      let it shine, *(3 times)*
   Let it shine, let it shine, let it shine.

This Ol' Hammer

Work Song

With heavy hammer strokes

1. This ol' ham-mer_____ killed John Hen-ry,_____

— This ol' ham-mer_____ killed John Hen-ry,_____

— This ol' ham-mer_____ killed John Hen-ry,_____

But it can't kill me,_____ it can't kill me._____

2. Take this hammer to the Captain, *(3 times)*
   Tell him I'm gone,
   tell him I'm gone.

3. If he asks you what's the matter, *(3 times)*
   Tell him you don't know,
   tell him you don't know.

4. If he asks you was I running, *(3 times)*
   Tell him no!
   tell him no!

Who Built the Ark? Noah, Noah

Call and response

Refrain
Who built the ark....

5. Now in come the animals two by two,
   Hippopotamus and kangaroo.

6. Now in come the animals three by three,
   Two big cats and a bumblebee.

7. Now in come the animals four by four,
   Two through the window and two through the door.

8. Now in come the animals five by five,
   Four little sparrows and the redbird's wife.

   Refrain
   Who built the ark....

9. Now in come the animals six by six,
   Elephant laughed at the monkey's tricks.

10. Now in come the animals seven by seven,
    Four from home and the rest from heaven.

11. Now in come the animals eight by eight,
    Some were on time and the others were late.

12. Now in come the animals nine by nine,
    Some was a-shouting and some was a-crying.

    Refrain
    Who built the ark....

13. Now in come the animals ten by ten,
    Five black roosters and five black hens.

14. Now Noah says, go shut that door,
    The rain's started dropping and we can't take more.

    Refrain
    Who built the ark....

White Coral Bells

Sweetly

1. White cor - al bells up - on a slen - der stalk,

Lil - lies of the val - ley deck my gar - den walk.

2. Oh, don't you wish that you could hear them ring?
   That will happen only when the fairies sing.